I Am Kind
By Aaron Fields

Copyright © 2025 Aaron Fields. All rights reserved.

Published by The Write Perspective, LLC

All rights reserved. No part of this book shall be reproduced or transmitted in any form or by any means, electronic, mechanical, magnetic, photographic including photocopying, recording or by any information storage and retrieval system, without prior written permission of the publisher. No copyright liability is assumed with respect to the use of the information contained in this book. Even though every precaution has been taken in preparation for this book, the publisher/author assumes no responsibility for errors or omissions. Neither is any liability assumed for any damage that results from the use of the information in this book.

ISBN: 978-1-953962-57-7

Kindness doesn't have to be big to be powerful..

In I Am Kind, meet Amina—a warm-hearted child who learns that kindness can be quiet, simple, and brave. From helping a new classmate to comforting her little brother, Amina shows that every act of kindness counts.

This gentle and inclusive story celebrates everyday empathy and connection. With practical tips for parents and joyful illustrations, this book helps children build strong, kind hearts—one story at a time.

This is Amina.
She loves smiling at people—even strangers.
It makes their day a little brighter.

Every day, Amina finds a way to be kind.

At school, Amina saw someone sitting alone.
Their eyes looked sad.

So she picked up her tray and said,
"Can I sit here?"
That was kind.

After recess, her classmate tripped and spilled his crayons.

Amina helped pick them up.
One by one.
That was kind too.

At home, her brother felt grumpy.
He didn't want to share the couch.

So Amina offered him her favorite blanket.
That helped.
Kindness can be quiet.

At the park, a little kid couldn't reach the water fountain.

Amina called her dad to help.
Kindness is asking too.

Later, her friend gave her a hug.
Amina felt so much love.

**Kindness can be small, soft, or brave.
It lives inside your heart.**

Amina is kind.
And guess what?
You are too.

"Why KIND Matters"

Kindness is one of the first social-emotional skills children develop. Practicing kindness helps kids build empathy, friendship, and emotional awareness.

Your child learns kindness through modeling, praise, and everyday opportunities to help others.

Praise Tip: Instead of saying, "You're such a nice kid," try, "It was kind of you to share your toy."

Try These at Home:

Make a family "kindness jar" to collect kind acts.

Role-play situations where your child can help others.

Catch kindness in action and praise it with specifics.

www.ingramcontent.com/pod-product-compliance
Lightning Source LLC
Chambersburg PA
CBHW041633040426
42446CB00024B/3495